The Godmen

LUKE JOHNSON

ISBN 978-93-5458-164-9
Copyright © Luke Johnson, 2021

First published in India 2021 by Leadstart Inkstate
A Division of One Point Six Technologies Pvt Ltd

119-123, 1st Floor, Building J2, B - Wing,
Wadala Truck Terminal, Wadala East,
Mumbai 400022, Maharashtra, INDIA
Phone: +91 96999 33000
Email: info@leadstartcorp.com
www.leadstartcorp.com

Disclaimer: The views expressed in this book are those of the Author and do not pertain to be held by the Publisher.

Editor: Vaibhav Pathare
Cover: R. Maharaja
Layouts: Kshitij Dhawale

I would like to dedicate this book to all of the godmen who have failed to deliver their promises.

About the Author

I am a certified IT Technician and had formerly worked in Europe within the computing industry. I am now employed within the healthcare sector. My career now involves doing the finances of numerous employees.

I enjoy reading books especially on philosophy, religion, and in particular on the neurology of consciousness. The nature and origin of consciousness is such a complex matter that nobody really knows much about; this is what makes it so interesting, I guess for many. My favourite books and articles on consciousness are the ones written by Sir Roger Penrose, Stuart Hameroff, Donald Hoffman, and Anil Seth.

I am an avid computer programmer, often programming in C/C++, Pascal, Visual Basic, and Assembly Language. In my spare time, I like to cycle, walk, and listen to various types of music. I usually cycle and walk to keep fit and stay healthy. My musical interests range from classical, ambient, pop to intelligent drum 'n' bass and pretty much everything else that is melodious. I have been entranced by melodic music from a very young age. I do therefore go and see it performed live locally and nationally.

Acknowledgements

I would like to thank my publisher for taking on my work and turning it into a reality. And without the profound work of Father Joseph Mahoney on Multiple Personality Disorder, this book would have not been possible for me to write.

Contents

INTRODUCTION

The number of godmen, who claim to have the power to remove demons, has increased considerably over the past few decades. Thus, exorcisms are now much more common in virtually every religion or faith than ever before – for treating the problems that any other conventional method has failed to do so.

The most likely candidates who undergo an exorcism are not necessarily those who believe in demons. On the contrary, it tends to be the ones who are stuck in a dead-end and not getting anywhere in life. Thanks to our modern science and medicine for this is now the prevalent norm. In dire situations, when people are stuck hopelessly and not getting anywhere, they will turn to someone else for help and advice. And godmen are now all over the place to provide that service at a cost. The only place you will not find them is in Antarctica. The temperature there seems to interfere with their power.

Demonic possession is acknowledged when a person has reached a very low point in their life. The process by which it occurs, and affects someone to that degree of misery, is known as *toona* in one particular mystical but dark religion. *Toona* basically means black magic, especially of a kind where a demon has been fed to someone in the form of their food, for which the term 'have been fed a thing' is used to describe it. There are also other terms for it but they all more or less mean the same thing in the end.

Toona is done insidiously by a jealous relative who wishes to inflict misfortune upon another relative. It is carried out intentionally to harm, if not to kill, the most loathed family member. Tales of such acts and deaths are often heard amongst the superstitious communities that reside within this country and across the rest of the world. So as a precaution, people can be seen consuming only half of what they have been given by or at their relatives. Others may be found doing a short prayer before eating or drinking anything. Prevention as they say is always better than cure.

Alternatively, a demon can become attached to someone by means of a curse or by being present in a place where such an entity exists. For example, a person can get possessed by being present in a graveyard. Graveyards are notorious for occupying the spirits of the dead night and day. An attached demon is however said to be less harmful than that of a consumed one. This is because it does not bond to the internal organs of a person's body. Whether this is true or not is something that nobody really knows for certain and probably never will. But maybe it is a matter left aside for the Christian Deliverance Study Group to ascertain for us. Nevertheless, Christians tend to believe in the attached and not in the other. They do however believe that a demon can enter through the mouth of a person, but this is not to be regarded as a consumed one. In other religions or faiths, these types of demonic possession may be referred to as ju-ju, sihr, voodoo magic, witchcraft, or even something else nastier.

Besides being able to kill someone off, demons can also cause many other problems: most of them being mental whilst some of them being physical. For instance, they can cause aggression, anxiety, depression, psychosis, schizophrenia, poverty, insecurity, addiction, abuse, bruising, suicide, etc. They can also cause pains and aches, headaches and migraines, distressing thoughts or dreams, forgetfulness, or confusion. But in the majority of cases, they will always prevent someone from achieving or succeeding in something. Thus, much of what they can do, will hinder or ruin a person's education, employment, friendship, relationship, migration (to a better country), happiness, intelligence, righteousness (to be virtuous), prosperity, ownership (of a property or belonging), and so on. Demons are therefore said to prevent the progression of someone's life for the worst. This is a predicament, of someone's life, which the empirical sciences have completely failed to solve, and thus have left it for others to try and fix; hence, why we have apostles, priests, saints, vicars, astrologers, clairvoyants, herbalists, mediums, mystics, numerologists, palmists, psychics, psychometrists, tarotists, babas, fakirs, gurus, imams, mahants, pujaris, pundits, sants, swamis, charlatans, fakers, prigs, quacks, deliverance ministers, exorcists, witches, etc., to deal with what the doctors and the specialists have ignored altogether. The term 'doctors and specialists' is used specifically throughout this text to allude to the experts who work within the health and medical sector.

Regardless of the variety of demons there are, and the harm that they can do to somebody, there is not a single shred of evidence to suggest that they do really exist on our planet. Maybe they do somewhere else in the universe but, to make someone believe in their illusive existence here is the job of the godman. The godmen are apparently too good at doing this because of their skill in trickery – that which is about to be revealed henceforth.

Victims of exorcisms should never be afraid of an exorcist.

One

THE EXORCISM

It must be said now that the godman Mahant Jaspal Kapoor Kalia Ji Maharaj, has been exorcizing other people with problems, at his grand temple for over three decades since its opening. Whatever he did prior to this is unknown.

Before expounding on the righteous work of Mahant Kalia Ji herein, it is important to note that, the main prayer at the temple, during when most of the congregation is present, takes place every Sunday morning at eleven o'clock. On all other days, it is at seven o'clock in the evening, and whereof Tuesday evenings are the most popular. The time on Sundays is unique: it gives plenty of time for the followers to get to the temple from wherever they are in the country. Sunday's is also special because it is a holy day allocated for the god Baba Balak Nath, and Tuesday's likewise for the goddess Mata. The goddess Mata has many manifestations of Her existence. Her name when spoken represents them all verbally but, it is hardly ever used textually. The word Mata, when it is not used as Her name, is a formal title for a priestess. This can be either textual or verbal.

The chief exorcism at the temple is conducted every Saturday evening between the hours of seven-thirty and nine. It involves drinking and vomiting an excessive quantity of (holy) water which contains ash and/or milk. The water is supplied in a big plastic bottle and refilled by someone when it gets empty; drank repeatedly with a steel glass until it causes nausea, then vomited back out into a large plastic bowl that is suitably provided for it. No solid food can be consumed for several hours prior to or during this sickly activity. Otherwise, it will all come out of the stomach of the doer with the repetitive drinking and vomiting of water. This form of hydro-exorcism, in which twenty or so will participate in at the weekend on an empty stomach, along with members of their family to support/encourage them through it, is appropriately called the *sick method*. The water that is used in this method for drinking and vomiting, washes out the (consumed) demon from within the body of the participant. The time that it can take for it to wash it out completely can be from a couple of weeks to several months – if lucky. However, the demon is always washed out bit by bit and very slowly with the *sick method*. It does therefore take over a year or so to wash it out entirely.

Often it is the case, where one participant is compelled by another to compete with each other, whilst sitting down on the floor uncomfortably for about an hour and a half, just to drink and vomit as much amount of water, to wash out their demon more quickly than what is actually anticipated by the *sick method*. But there was an incident once when one weak male individual had fainted on the floor because he drank and vomited too much (holy) water. Luckily, he was taken to the local hospital in an ambulance, where the doctors and specialists treated him for his unconscious condition. Afterwards, everyone at the temple had speculated that his demon was going to take his life away when he had fainted, but Mahant Kalia Ji had instead saved him from his death with the power of God, yet no one in the hospital ever became privy to this speculation of about him from anyone in the temple; which is why everything nonsensical about the temple remains still buried so deep in silence.

Many also bathe with the water and the ash which Mahant Kalia Ji provides at the temple to take home, again to speed things up even more. After all, who wants to drink and vomit for years on end every weekend and wretchedly to get better? So, people do have high hopes of being miraculously cured with the *sick method;* from the problems that they are made to believe, or know for certain, cannot be solved by any of the doctors or specialists out there. Yet they carry on taking the medications that are prescribed by them to alleviate their existing pains and difficulties. But the medications that they take have only enough power to keep them alive in their misery. So, what benefits does medicine really bring to those who are hoping for a miracle to occur?

Most nights during the exorcism, pungent smoke from off the embers in a pan is waved in front of the possessed person to make the demon within them *play*. Sometimes, the aromatic smoke from off-lit incense is used for the same purpose. Towards the end of the smoky exorcism, whoever is partaking in it, or supporting/encouraging them through it, will have to make a monetary donation in a circular stainless-steel tray for in return a blessing from a lit ghee filled lamp.

When everybody has been blessed by the lamp, the money that is donated as of it in the tray only amounts to a beneficial tip for Mahant Kalia Ji. Shortly after the tip, the emetic session on the Saturday is brought to its closure for the night and until the next one on again at the ensuing weekend. Finally, the huge pile of sick in the bowls gets poured down the loo, by the ones who would be now too tired and hungry to do it – though they do get to have some rest and supper after doing it. Thereafter, it is incumbent on everyone to stay overnight at the temple and sleep on the floor.

Sleeping on the floor is intended to address the god Baba Balak Nath in the night and reciprocally benefit the sleepers in the long run, particularly in their next incarnation.

On the next day, the sleepers are obliged to get up early and then buy some *roat*[1] and *parshad*[2] in the morning. The *roat* and *parshad* are both made and sold to the public in the temple on a Sunday. When they are bought, the *roat* must be offered to the god Baba Balak Nath and the *parshad* to the goddess Mata. The offering of these foods to the deities at their designated altar in the temple is an essential part of the service for the divine. The money paid for them is a blessing unto Mahant Kalia Ji. The Kingdom of God, for the hapless possessed and their supporters, does therefore have its commercial price.

Mahant Kalia Ji also uses a *touching method* to perform an exorcism at the temple. That method is used by him in addition to the *sick* one and on other days but not every time. It involves Mahant Kalia Ji touching the head of a possessed person with a pair of large metal tongs, or with a bunch of peacock feathers – on either a Tuesday, Thursday, Saturday, or Sunday. Touching the head with one of the objects, causes the touched

1   A sweet flat bread circular cake.
2   A sweet flour (semolina) and ghee-based food.

person to vomit out their *playing* demon into a glass bottle. When the demon has been vomited out in that sentient fashion, the bottle is thrown away afterwards by someone and into a nearby flowing river or stream, with its top back on, and with a heavy brick tied to it – for of course to make it sink and drown.

In a Christian deliverance, the Bible or the cross is used in a similar way to the pair of large metal tongs or the bunch of peacock feathers; but the person is never made to vomit out their demon into a glass bottle. With the Bible, or the cross, the demon is struck to suffer in pain, and thus to make it leave through the mouth or from the body of its host. The other alternative object to the Bible is the Koran in Islam; but as to what that is capable of doing, shall be left over for the keen reader of this book to discern. There are also other objects for exorcizing besides these: a flower or an amulet, for example, can be used to ward off or remove (attached) evil spirits. These handy items are however less important and merely act as placebos. Despite their insignificance, the flower (for bathing), and the amulet (for wearing); along with the Bible, the cross, and the Koran; all contain the power of God to remove a demon – or to heal someone. The same sort of godly power also exists within the stuff that Mahant Kalia Ji uses: the lit ghee-filled lamp and the *roat* and *parshad* in the exorcism. Just how much power they all contain will become transparent as we move on.

Many exorcists like Mahant Kalia Ji will also sprinkle (holy) water onto the face of the person whose demon is *playing*. Sprinkling the water on them helps to purify their (unholy) body and punish the demon within it. Exorcists are poised to do this repeatedly and in front of their intrigued audience to show them the power of God against evil. And seeing one do it on someone whose demon is *playing* should leave you standing speechless with the belief in God upon when their demon screams aloud in hysteria.

There are periods when the demon will expose itself by shaking the head and spinning the arms round rapidly of the possessed person, whilst swinging their body across with a force and energy that even Newton or Einstein could have never comprehended with their mathematical lingua – all for to scream out loud that it is not coming out of the body. The demon may also speak out the name of the person by whom it was fed or cursed when it has exposed itself fully – that's if the exorcist threatens it to say it then. However, this is not something that happens to everyone in the exorcism; nor does everyone experience the exposure of the demon during it. Therefore, it is the case of it happening to some and not to others.

The exposure of the demon is known as the 'thing is playing'. In a Christian deliverance, it's known as the 'demon is rising' (from the dead). In other religions or faiths, it may be called something else. For the purpose of unambiguity, it will be referred to as *playing* throughout this entire text.

Playing is believed to be precipitated by when the demon within a person encounters something divine, like for example, the presence of a god or the power of a godman. Unfortunately, this held belief about the precipitation of *playing* is not absolutely true in whichever religion or faith an exorcism is administered. Spirit release therapists, who have no supernatural powers whatsoever, will use hypnosis to make the spirits in their clients *play*. *Playing* is also associated with the subjects of dissociative states: the dissociative identity of a subject is the demon in an exorcism.

A demon should stop *playing* once it has been extracted from a person by an exorcist. Surprisingly, for the odd one, this is not true. An exorcism does therefore have its strange flaws. One man's demon had started *playing* unexpectedly in him, which Mahant Kalia Ji had removed from his body many years ago. How this was possible, contradicted the very essence of an exorcism and still does to even this day. In other words, the same old demon should not be *playing* again in a person once it has been expelled from them for good. But if the outcome of an exorcism can be flawed like it is depicted here, then surely *playing* must be a type of dissociative behaviour rather than anything else. Thus, it cannot be precipitated by anything godly or even something powerful. Could the aim of an exorcism be then to stop a person from dissociating altogether and not to remove any kind of demonic spirit?

The skill of making someone *play* can be learnt slowly by carefully watching an exorcist who has it. There have been some who have done this at the temple to become exorcists themselves somewhere else. That is why the number of them is always increasing to heal the sick with what they claim to be the power of God. As a result of this claim in the power of God, it becomes the time when Mahant Kalia Ji, clad in orange, threatens or beats up the *playing* demon in a person with a pair of large metal tongs – in order to force it out from their body. The metallic beatings do in turn hurt and bruise; yet everyone who likes to watch them inflicted upon someone is totally brainwashed into thinking that they do not harm the possessed but only the demon within the stricken person. And as of the painful beatings with the pair of large metal tongs, the screams of the *playing* demon would inevitably turn into shrills. Other exorcists may prefer to use a stick to beat or their hands to slap for to also achieve this barbaric effect.

One lady was beaten to hell by Mahant Kalia Ji whilst her demon was *playing* aggressively in front of him. As a result of her beatings, she was left shrieking out loudly even after her demon had stopped *playing.* If Mahant Kalia Ji had carried on demonstrating the power of God to everyone then, she probably would have died therefrom. Alas, this is what had happened to Maricica Irina Cornici by someone else deadlier in a different place of worship. Proceeding on from where we were before this tragedy, another person had ended up with a black eye across his face because of his beatings at the temple. Now, on what grounds can this torture be ever morally right? Moreover, where is the law to protect the most vulnerable from the harmful practices of godmen?

Mahant Kalia Ji is very skilful in choosing who he exorcizes at the temple: he picks out only the attendees who are susceptible to the belief of demonic possession and can be easily managed by him. Every other exorcist does this skilfully as well in their sacred institution, to exploit who they can perpetually. Anyone who they cannot is completely rejected for the doctors and specialists to treat in vain.

Some of the people that Mahant Kalia Ji had exorcized are now dead and forgotten. At the Love of God Community in Birmingham, a similar sort of thing had also happened to a few by a couple of wild Christians and with their deadly sticks. Since that place has now been defunct from a long time ago, we shall never really know how the possessed had died from thereat. But most of the other people that Mahant Kalia Ji had exorcized: have thus disappeared from the temple in silence. Just a few, therefore, remain attending. So how Mahant Kalia Ji has healed someone miraculously remains yet to be seen. Godmen have somehow managed to shield themselves from being asked this at all, so the truth about them never really comes out. Only that they have healed thousands end up being heard publicly, from time to time and from place to place, for bringing hope to those who need help which others cannot provide. Wherefore do we then have the doctors and specialists if they cannot bring any hope to their patients like the godmen can?

Overall, it is the exorcism which makes the onlookers believe that, Mahant Kalia Ji has been blessed with the Almighty power to heal the sick. Ultimately, this is what incites them to bestow their money at him in the name of God; hence, the exorcism is just bait for his income and status, which nobody ever realizes.

Without anybody ever realizing this, Mahant Kalia Ji carries on getting richer and richer, whilst his demonic victims, carry on getting sicker and vomiter. Amidst this oblivion of financial gain and loss, Mahant Kalia Ji keeps no record of those he has exorcized or is exorcizing now. Exorcists have a bad habit of leaving this responsibility to their all-knowing deities. Evidence of their work is therefore non-existent. The possessed, who are oblivious to this void, do not in respect inform their doctor that they are undergoing an exorcism somewhere. Who would believe them if they did tell? For some unknown reason, Mahant Kalia Ji has never exorcized members of his own relatives with the methods that he uses on other people. Perhaps he believes that their own doctor can provide better health care for them than he can.

No godman should ever go unchallenged.

Two

THE CHONKI

Besides the exorcism, Mahant Kalia Ji also practises the *chonki,* the *gathi*, and the *keel*. The *chonki* is when he, if not his partner sometimes, possesses the spirit of a deity. During the *chonki*, Mahant Kalia Ji will be in an altered state of consciousness. That state of consciousness is very similar to that of a demon *playing* in a person, though it tends to be less chaotic but far more dominant and eloquent than the demon. More importantly, the transition of the state from Mahant Kalia Ji's and to that of the deity occurs when Mahant Kalia Ji is focusing on it, and by doing some deep meditation in the temple. The transition of it can also be spontaneous sometimes. It can therefore occur without Mahant Kalia Ji doing anything meditative and focal.

Fundamentally, the *chonki* is the divine possession of a deity, whereas *playing* is the demonic possession of a demon. But the *chonki* in contrast to *playing* is accompanied by the mesmeric chants of the deity; their mesmeric effect is akin to the hypnosis in a spirit release therapy, or the pungent smoke from off the embers in a pan.

If the tongue of Mahant Kalia Ji pops out during the *chonki*, then it will be the goddess Mata present in him, whereupon a red veil will be worn over his head to signify Her presence. Otherwise, it will be the god Baba Balak Nath present in his body. The term 'Baba Ji's *chonki*', or 'Mata Ji's *chonki*', is used thereupon to identify which deity is present in the body. The popping out of the tongue during Mata Ji's *chonki*, denotes Her wrath against the sins of humankind.

On the odd occasion, a member of the congregation may be found doing the *chonki* spontaneously at the temple instead of Mahant Kalia Ji (or his partner). This finding should not be regarded as something unusual. Apart from Mahant Kalia Ji (or his partner), there are other men and women who are able to do the *chonki*. Not all of them attend the temple, as their own home is usually more than suffice to execute it in with ease and without any fear.

The *chonki* is performed at the temple every Sunday afternoon, between the hours of one and four. On a Tuesday and Thursday evening, it is practised between eight o'clock and ten o'clock. Sometimes the *chonki* is conducted on a Saturday during the *sick method*. When it is carried out then, the demons will be *playing* out violently, because of the mesmeric presence of a deity.

The presence of the Deity[†], which would be normally of the god Baba Balak Nath in Mahant Kalia Ji's body, can be very strong on the *chonki*: He has the shear strength to beat out the *playing* demons with a pair of large metal tongs – on it. The sight of that horrific beating in an exorcism, wherever it may be for the confounded observer, is what makes them believe in the power of God. The more the people believe in the power of God, the more popular the *chonki* thereby becomes – often by word-of-mouth.

Today, the *chonki* is the main attraction that draws the public to the temple. It is what lures in the people from all over to serve the Deity. Distinguished university lectures will also come in the temple sometimes with their inquisitive students but to show them what it is all about. This is definitely useful for any learner who is studying religion as their prime subject and especially at a deeper level. But for others who need some help and advice, the *chonki* is primarily the time when the Deity provides faith healing to the public. Consequently, about a dozen or so will arrive in the temple for it, from near or afar, and alone or with their close relatives. Optimistically they will await in the temple, from about the time of the main prayer, and

---

[†]   Most of the times on the *chonki*, the Deity is the god Baba Balak Nath (He) and not the goddess Mata (She).

acquire the healing when the *chonki* is in progression.

Part of faith healing is to determine whether someone is possessed or not. Sometimes this is very easy to do, especially when the demon within a person starts to *play* in front of the Deity or somewhere else in the temple. At other times, a person is judged as being possessed if the Deity says so. Another part of faith healing, which is beyond the realm of science and medicine, is to establish if the problem of someone is due to some wrongdoings in their past life. How the Deity is able to do this is beyond the scope of even Himself to explain it. And if you want to know what the rest of faith healing is about, well, it can be discovered quite easily by asking the relevant university lectures or their academic students.

During the *chonki*, or as they say on the *chonki*, the (omnipotent) Deity will enunciate several boons, often by sitting on the most comfortable cushion that man could have ever made. The cushion is very similar to the one that His Holiness Brahmrishi Shree Kumar Swami Ji sits on all day but never so in Syria or Somalia.

Thus, with respect to the strategic posture of His Holiness, godmen do seem to know how to stay away from danger, or starvation, on this Earth. By knowing how to do this comfortably somewhere, it is only then that they are able to do something extraordinary with their powers. Remarkably, a boon is thereby when the Deity summons someone over to the *chonki* by enunciating their problem. It therefore allows a supplicant to come forward to the Deity and to speak to Him about their problem. The supplicant is also entitled to do this, if they need to, with the company of their relatives. However, before someone can speak to the Deity about their problem, they will have to make a monetary donation unto Him and by bowing down to His feet, on after having come forward to Him on the *chonki*. The donation at that precious moment in time can be from a mere euro to as much as infinity. After making it with respect and bowing, it is thenceforth permissible by tradition for the supplicant to speak to the Deity.

When a supplicant has spoken to the Deity about their problem, and then departed away from Him back to where they were originally in the temple, if there are any more awaiting therein with the alike problem, then they would have to also come forward to Him successively and speak about it. Otherwise, the Deity will enunciate the next boon, which would be different from the previous one, and for the problem of someone else in the temple. This cycle of enunciation from the Deity will continue until the *chonki* has collapsed (ended). At the point of its collapse, Mahant Kalia Ji will return to his own state of consciousness and become himself.

When the Deity enunciates a boon on the *chonki*, it is claimed to be in accord with the problem of someone who is present in the temple. Let us say then the Deity enunciates the following boon on it: "The one who has pains in their body." Firstly, this boon would mean: someone who has pains in their body is present in the temple, and the Deity is absolutely aware of their presence. Secondly, they need to come forward to Him for a solution to their problem.

According to the public who frequent the temple, the Deity does not take a guess, but foresees for certain the problem of someone who is present in the temple, when enunciating a boon for them on the *chonki*. From their point of view: He already knows everything about everyone and at all times – even about you and me. Although their belief in Him is very plausible, there are still the odd moments when no one will come forward to the Deity after Him having enunciated a boon for someone in the temple. On those odd moments, the enunciated boon of the Deity does not concord with the problem of someone present in the temple. As to why this happens then will be the utmost duty of Professor Ron Geaves to find out.

In general, the boons of the Deity are aimed at the people who have no solution to their problem. Collectively, they are intended for the public who cannot progress or succeed in life – just as what the exorcism is for at the temple. This is a wonderful solution but one which cannot be bestowed upon those who are anaemic, arthritic, asthmatic, autistic, diabetic, epileptic, limbless, homeless, famished, malnourished, dispersed, etc. The reason it cannot be bestowed upon them is because the (omnipotent) Deity never enunciates the boons on the *chonki* to solve their problems. But does this neglect of His, in turn, imply that He does not have the power to help everyone?

Anyway, a supplicant is considered to very lucky if their problem coincides with the boon enunciated by the Deity, as it gives them an opportunity to get it solved from someone who knows a lot more about it than anyone else. The expertise of the Deity, in solving (complex) problems, in relation to health and wellbeing, is always reckoned to be superior to that of any (hopeless) doctor or specialist. No wonder why people turn to Him when nothing else works for them. It must be therefore stated here, of about the status quo, that science and medicine has not yet fixed what it had set out to do from a very long time ago.

The Deity takes a unique approach on the *chonki* to tackle the problem of someone. It is made up of granting rituals in an easy manner and to the summoned supplicant who comes forward and speaks to Him. The rituals, which can be repetitive and/or tedious to do, are granted by the Deity to help that person get better. This is analogous to a doctor prescribing medicine to a patient in the surgery. On the *chonki*, however, the prescription would be slightly different to that of a doctor: an employer who is struggling financially with his business maybe told by the Deity to light a ghee filled lamp in his home on a weekly basis and to buy some *roat* and *parshad* in the temple every weekend, for to boost his earnings. Simply by doing these prescribed rituals indefinitely, the employer will be serving the Deity in return to gain prosperity from Him. Unfortunately, this is not a remedy that a doctor (or a specialist) could prescribe to someone in the surgery; surely the Deity must therefore have an advantage over science and medicine when it comes to making someone better off.

The rituals of the Deity are vital in healing the public at the temple. Rejecting them, or forgetting to do them, or even not doing them properly, would mutually provide nothing to the conferred supplicant. Occasionally, the Deity does declare this on the *chonki*. Upon hearing that ilk of declaration, what choice does anyone have then to get what they want in life? Whoever has been let down by everyone else should know the answer to this question without any doubt.

Other than granting rituals on the *chonki*, the Deity also uses the *touching method,* to heal, or to exorcize someone at the temple. Albeit, no glass bottle is required for vomiting anything into upon the healing from the Deity, as it is carried out only on a person who is not *playing,* or is either devoid of a demon. The glass bottle is only used in an exorcism to put a demon into it with the *touching method;* whereas the healing from the Deity is only carried out on someone who needs to be just healed from it.

With the *touching method*, the power of Deity is transferred through one of the objects and onto the person who needs to be healed or exorcized by it. Whilst listening to some relaxation music in a safe place, spiritual healers can also heal (not exorcize) someone by transferring the healing energy from a Higher Being or Source. They would do the transfer of energy for the healing by using their magical hands. Christians on the other hand use prayers in their monumental churches to heal somebody. This is known as *prayer healing.* Sikhs sometimes do the same in their golden gurudwaras but probably not on Hindus. Plus, they do not perform any exorcisms on anyone.

Volunteering regularly at the temple is also obligated by the (rewarding) Deity. This is necessary to promote healing and to serve Him rightly. Serving the Deity also means serving Mahant Kalia Ji – from by which Mahant Kalia Ji gains his subservient disciples and therapeutic masseurs; but who after years of serving him, for to have a better life and future, end up never coming back to the temple again.

Sometimes the (benign) Deity will preach on the *chonki*. This will happen when the moment is right. And when the moment is right, silence will fall upon the temple. The wrath of the Deity will then speak. The ears of the congregation will then open wide. Someone amongst them will then become the condemned victim of the wrath of the Deity.

The wrath of the Deity can be very oppressive on the *chonki*; as far as no one ever dares to question His power to heal anyone. One senile man was coerced in fury by the Deity, to accept that he was cured of his slightly disabled leg (with the *sick method*) when in fact he was not. Without objecting to the wrongful coercion of the Deity, he was left bowing down to Him instead and begging for His forgiveness in humiliation, but never to be seen or heard in the temple again. The wrath of the Deity can also be intimidating; whereby, He had threatened an entire congregation to buy some *roat* and *parshad* on a certain day at the temple. The threat was proposed by Him thence for to forestall any bad luck upon them. Although it was a clever trick and guess what for – the congregation still went to the temple and bought the damn *roat* and *parshad* on that day. Again, the money paid for the foods at that time but in this case, by the frightened congregation, did go to Mahant Kalia Ji eventually. It was probably finagled for his yearly pilgrimages to India but by means of a (benign) threat.

When the *chonki* has collapsed, Mahant Kalia Ji will hand out blessed cardamom pods, threads, amulets, flowers, incense, etc., to take home, and to heal someone. Just like the duration of the *sick method,* the healing from these objects, individually or collectively, can also take a very long time to attain: years rather than months or even weeks – if unlucky. However, that miracle of healing never really happens to anyone in the end with such things. What happens instead is this: a potent placebo effect will transpire at some point in time, and make the person believe that they have been miraculously cured of their problem, by the power of God, when in fact they have not. Faith healing of this kind, therefore, only rearranges the thoughts of someone's mind and not the state of someone's health; yet it carries on being regarded as the work of miracles and not the work of tricksters, no matter what religion or faith it is practised in.

On a rare occasion, the Deity can be seen exorcizing Mahant Kalia Ji on the *chonki*, whilst being present in his body. Whenever this rarity occurs, the demon within his body is vomited out immediately into a glass bottle; yet it can take Mahant Kalia Ji ages to remove that of someone else's with the *sick method*. Why is this the case for others and not for him you may ask? Well, the answer to this question is resolved by how much faith a person has in the Deity. Mahant Kalia Ji is regarded as having the most, so his demon is always removed much more quickly than that of any other. The others are regarded as having the least, so their demon is always removed much more slowly than that of Mahant Kalia Ji's. The notion of how much faith a person has in the Deity also applies to the supplicants who have been granted a boon on the *chonki*. In fact, the whole principle of faith healing in every religion or faith is based on this type of notion. Therefore, the more faith a person has in something divine, the more chance that he (or she) will have in getting better. Otherwise, nothing will happen to them at all. Ironically, the power of an exorcist is measured by how fast they can remove a demon from someone who hardly has any faith. On the basis of this verity, who exactly is then the most powerful exorcist in the world? Could it be the late Reverend Gabriele Amorth in Italy? He had allegedly performed over a hundred and sixty thousand exorcisms in his life but factually never one on a possessed suicidal bomber. Otherwise, it could be the Apostle Trevor Newport in the United Kingdom. Compare to the Italian one, he has done countless miracles of healing with the power of God (but not when so many have terribly died due to the current coronavirus pandemic). Frankly, he claims that he has cured people of cancers, blindness, and disabilities. The Evangelist Vincent Jan ten Bouwhuis, in a dandier style than any other exorcist, has also done something amazing with his godly powers.

Evidently, the Deity has never demonstrated anything miraculous on the *chonki*. Nothing even suggests that He is really a god when present in Mahant Kalia Ji's body. Instead, He seems to be something else and very deceptive of it. Theoretically, this should be obvious to everyone, but in reality, it is not. Hopefully, the following incident should alter this perception of the many and bring about the true nature of the *chonki* with much more clarity hereupon: an insightful moment of eureka had occurred one day when the (omniscient) Deity had made a false statement about and to one His loyal adherents, who had believed that He knew everything about him. Consequently, that adherent has not been back to the temple since that day. Had he therefore witnessed then what was literally a hoax in a holy place, from by simply hearing a misstatement about himself? If so, then under what circumstances could the *chonki* at the temple be a genuine possession of a Supreme Being? Moreover, how can we now find out who had assassinated John Fitzgerald Kennedy if the (omniscient) Deity is a liar?

In most cases, it is easier for a person who is prone to *playing* to learn how to do the *chonki* than of any other. The *chonki* can also be learnt over time by carefully watching a godman perform it. There have been a few who have done this, again at the temple, to become godmen themselves somewhere else. That is why the number of them is always increasing to heal the sick with what they claim to be the possession of God. But their claim in the possession of God is only a skill for making money out of the sick, which Doctor Emma Cohen is not even aware of in Oxfordshire. Thus, another man who has taken up this skill to a satisfying pecuniary level is of course the godman at the magnificent Ek Niwas Universal Divine Temple. It is the case of if someone else can do it then so can I.

Who does more harm: the living or the dead?

Three

THE GATHI, THE KEEL, AND THE MONEY

Gathi is an exorcism on the deceased. It transmigrates their soul into its next life to prevent it from harming the related living in this life. A red veil is wrapped around a fresh coconut to initiate that transmigration at the temple. Elaborate incantations are then applied simultaneously to the two objects by Mahant Kalia Ji to attribute the soul of the deceased to the coconut. Once the soul has been attributed, the coconut must be kept held tiresomely from hereon in the hands of the bereaver, and until it reaches its destination many miles away. Thus, the coconut is taken away to India in a plane, along with Mahant Kalia Ji and his partner. There it is deposited, on after having done some prolonged rituals on it, into the part of the river Ganges which runs right through the city of Haridwar. That part of the river, even though it is seriously polluted, is considered to be the holy core for transmigrating the souls of the deceased. Ashes of the dead are always deposited there by the bereaved to perform the *gathi*. The coconut is therefore an alternative object to the ashes. The ashes are however said to be much more effective than the coconut because they are the real substance of the dead.

A *Gathi* List is furnished by Mahant Kalia Ji to get all the materials that are crucial for spiritual transmigration. A payment of about a thousand euros or more must also be made in advance to him to carry out the transmigrating exorcism in India. The cost is proportionally higher when there is more than one bereaver of the kindred participating in it. Furthermore, there are the additional monetary charges made by the many corrupt holy men in India for their exequies on the coconut to make some money. What a price then to pay for not to be haunted by those who are no longer alive and with us anymore. Flying back from India after the *gathi* has been completed has its burden too: the group of bereavers who take part in it for the sake of themselves and their families will have to carry in their heavy luggage the commodities which Mahant Kalia Ji buys in India and then sells back at the temple.

One poor lady, who was also doing the *sick method* at the temple, died a few months after she had done the *gathi* in India with her son. Her husband was already dead before her own death. The *gathi* was therefore meant for him when she was alive and he was dead. She was advised by Mahant Kalia Ji and his partner to perform it on his soul then for the sake of herself and her children. When she did do that, by also drinking and vomiting prior to it at the temple, the outcome was not as expected. Why?

Spiritualists have a positive alternative to the *gathi* if the death of that lady is too sad for you to think about. In lieu of what Mahant Kalia Ji (and his partner) can do powerfully in India, they will use their special hands to transfer the healing energy from the spirits of the dead, and onto the person who needs it – over here. Spirit release therapists have in comparison settled for releasing the spirits of the dead from within the bodies of the possessed. But by doing that, are they allowing the energy of the released spirits to be used by someone else on others? Here we have a question for which even the dead have no answer. Nonetheless, do check out the places where all of this is happening today. Plus, find out the prices to have it done to you or your loved one.

Not only can spirits coexist within someone's physical body but they can also roam around freely in someone's home. These kinds of roaming spirits, who can do a lot of harm with their negative energy, are known as ghosts. But unlike demons, ghosts cannot be consumed or become attached; and due to their limited function, they require a different sort of exorcism to boot them out. A one that targets them specifically is called *keel*.

Keel is purely an exorcism of the house, and it is usually practised more than once across a decade or so to rid the occupying ghosts. Several practices of *keel* are necessary because the initial few do not always work. Why they are a failure on the outset is a mystery to everyone. In spite of this perplexity, possibly because of mankind's ignorance, *keel* can be performed on its own, or before or after the *gathi*. It can also be an integral part of the *sick* or the *touching method*. Every now and then, Mahant Kalia Ji does utilize the whole shebang on his clients to obtain the desired placeboic effect on them.

The *keel* consists of Mahant Kalia Ji uttering incantations in the haunted house whilst the affected family are all present in it, and fumigating it by waving pungent smoke from off the embers in a pan – room by room. Plus, it involves Mahant Kalia Ji stapling the window frames, and the door frames, on the inside of the property. All the family of the same household must also stay overnight in the house for *keel* to be absolutely successful. Otherwise, the occupying ghosts will remain inside and carry on haunting them until they die. A *Keel* List, showing all the items that are required for the homely exorcism, is available from Mahant Kalia Ji.

In the name of Christ, Christian exorcists can also

remove ghosts from someone's home. If any information is required on their version of *keel*, even though it is not called that in Christianity, then do contact the appropriate Anglican exorcist about it. The Christian version should be in relation very similar to the one which Mahant Kalia Ji carries out over time, as all exorcisms are metaphorically the same underneath; so too are the godmen and their religious practices.

On the whole, participating in any of the exorcisms of Mahant Kalia Ji will necessitate adopting a Lacto-vegetarian diet, ideally for life. Furthermore, the consumption of alcohol, and lentils, is strictly forbidden with this dietary obligation. Wearing black clothing is also discouraged with the exorcisms, as it brings about bad luck and attracts the demons. Otherwise, punishment is deemed for transgression.

Godmen are certainly renowned for their super powers but hardly anything ever gets mentioned about their endless avarice. Pretty much all of them have their crafty ways of making (lots of) money out of someone and somewhere. The prominent investigator of the paranormal, James Randi, had exposed the empires of a few of them in his book on faith healers. That exposure had befallen the godmen in the distant past.

Now the time has come to do just the same, to some extent, on Mahant Kalia Ji.

Mahant Kalia Ji has several ways of making his money at the temple. Some of which are very deceptive. One that fits this description perfectly is when his dissociative state is pretending to be a god and then threatening the congregation to buy some *roat* and *parshad* in the temple. Another one, though less fearful, is by performing exorcisms on the souls of the deceased and then charging the troubled bereavers for his transmigrating work. Apart from this, Mahant Kalia Ji also sells various products in the temple to increase his income a bit more. One of the products is a picture of himself with a glowing halo around his head. The other ones include audio compact discs, video films, books, booklets, fabrics, flags (and their poles), incense, ornaments, statues, other pictures, etc. Furthermore, Mahant Kalia Ji will sing (along with his disciples) or perform *puja*[††] for families at a cost. A Puja List is provided by Mahant Kalia Ji to get all the things that are needed for the ritual.

A lot of Mahant Kalia Ji's money comes from the public donations that he receives in the temple, especially

---

[††]   A special kind of prayer, costing hundreds of euros and performed quickly for the whole family in the temple, sometimes in the name of their dead relative.

on the festivals Chet Chala Mela, Jagran, Mandir Anniversary, etc. The festivals are all celebrated at the temple, throughout the year and probably forever in eternity, to extol the god Baba Balak Nath or the goddess Mata. During the festive time, the temple is always full, if not overloaded with pious devotees. On the celebrations, they can be seen in there adorning Mahant Kalia Ji with flowers (to praise his godliness) and practically giving him money by bowing down to his feet (for perchance his mansion in India).

On a healthier spectrum than Mahant Kalia Ji (and his disciples), we have the Swami Baba Ramdev Ji with his awesome yogic stance far away. He too lives off public donations (and in peace); but whilst habitually denouncing the man-made flawed economical system, he has many followers and unofficial websites, promoting and selling expensive herbal remedies to the most deprived people in our society – hopefully, for to change the course of their life.

With his collection of sharp knives, the great John of God was also able to transform the life of someone but in his relaxing Casa. And now that he has been locked up, he can't seem to do anything great in a Prison Cell.

Despite the advances in science and medicine, the dependency on godmen is still on the rise.

BIBLIOGRAPHY

- **About Us**
  Trevor Newport Ministries
  https://trevornewport.com/about.htm

- **Baba Balak Nath Mandir**
  https://en-gb.facebook.com/Baba-Balak-Nath-Mandir-429017703808368/

- **Bhagwan Shri Laxmi Narayan Dham**
  Cosmic Grace
  https://cosmicgrace.org/

- **Child Abuse Linked to Accusations of "Possession" and "Witchcraft"**
  Eleanor Stobart
  Digital Education Resource Archive (DERA)
  https://dera.ioe.ac.uk/6416/1/RR750.pdf

- **Christian Deliverance Study Group**
  Charity Commission
  https://beta.charitycommission.gov.uk/charity-details?regid=1172851&subid=0

- **Demonic Possession or Mental Illness?**
  Beliefnet, Inc.
  *https://www.beliefnet.com/faiths/
  catholic/2000/09/demonic-possession-or-mental-
  illness.aspx*

- **Doctor Ashok's Ayurvedic Clinic**
  https://www.drashokayurveda.co.uk/

- **Ek Niwas Universal Divine Temple**
  https://www.ekniwas.net/

- **Exorcism Rituals: Effects on Multiple Personality
  Disorder Patients**
  George A Fraser
  University of Oregon Libraries
  *https://scholarsbank.uoregon.edu/xmlui/
  bitstream/handle/1794/1681/Diss_6_4_6_OCR_
  rev.pdf*

- **Faith Healing and Skepticism in Pakistan:
  Challenge and Instability.**
  Ryan Shaffer
  Skeptical Inquirer Magazine
  Committee for Skeptical Inquiry (CSI)
  *https://skepticalinquirer.org/2012/11/faith-
  healing-and-skepticism-in-pakistan-challenge-and-
  instability/*

- **FAQ's Healing**
  The Healing Trust
  https://www.thehealingtrust.org.uk/healing-faq/

- **Gabriele Amorth**
  Wikipedia, the free encyclopedia.
  https://en.wikipedia.org/wiki/Gabriele_Amorth

- **Healing and Deliverance**
  The Church of England – Birmingham
  http://www.cofebirmingham.com/hub/pastoral-care/healing-deliverance/

- **João Teixeira de Faria**
  Wikipedia, the free encyclopedia.
  https://en.wikipedia.org/wiki/Jo%C3%A3o_Teixeira_de_Faria

- **Mandir Baba Balak Nath**
  https://www.mandirbababalaknath.co.uk/

- **'Multiple Personality Disorder - Demons and Angels or Archetypal aspects of the inner self'**
  Doctor Haraldur Erlendsson
  Royal College of Psychiatrists
  https://www.rcpsych.ac.uk/docs/default-source/members/sigs/spirituality-spsig/spirituality-special-interest-group-publications-dr-haraldur-erlendsson-multiple-personality-disorder.pdf

- **Paranormal Occurrences and Deliverance Ministry**
  Diocese of Guildford
  https://www.cofeguildford.org.uk/about/explore/chaplaincies/paranormal-occurrences-and-deliverance-ministry

- **Peer Darbar**
  http://www.angelfire.com/blues2/psdahri/peer_darbar.html

- **Priest Jailed for Exorcism Death**
  BBC News
  http://news.bbc.co.uk/1/hi/world/europe/6376211.stm

- **Ramdev**
  Wikipedia, the free encyclopedia.
  https://en.wikipedia.org/wiki/Ramdev

- **Spirit Release Therapy**
  Inner Journeys
  http://www.innerjourneys.co.uk/spirit-release-therapy.html

- **Spiritualism**
  Wikipedia, the free encyclopedia.
  https://en.wikipedia.org/wiki/Spiritualism

- **The Legitimization of a Regional Folk Cult: The Transmigration of Baba Balaknath from Rural Punjab to Urban Europe**
  Ron Geaves and Catherine Geaves
  CrossAsia-Repository
  https://crossasia-repository.ub.uni-heidelberg.de/238/1/skanda.pdf

- **The Phenomenon of Possession and Exorcism in North India and Amongst the Punjabi Diaspora in Wolverhampton**
  Sandeep Singh Chohan
  CORE
  https://core.ac.uk/download/pdf/1932821.pdf

- **Vincent Bauhaus Ministries**
  https://www.bornagainministry.org/

- **What is Spirit Possession? Defining, Comparing, and Explaining Two Possession Forms**
  Emma Cohen
  University of Oxford
  http://users.ox.ac.uk/~soca0093/pdfs/CohenEthnos08.pdf

- **What Is Witchcraft Abuse?**
  AFRUCA
  http://www.afruca.org/wp-content/uploads/2013/06/SACUS05_What-is-witchcraft-abuse.pdf

- **Multiple Identities & False Memories: A Sociocognitive Perspective**
  Author: Nicholas P Spanos
  Publisher: American Psychological Association
  ISBN-13: 9781557988935

- **The Faith Healers**
  Author: James Randi
  Publisher: Prometheus Books
  ISBN-13: 9780879753696

FURTHER INFORMATION

- **Anomalistic Psychology Research Unit**
  https://www.gold.ac.uk/apru/

- **Asian Rationalist Society of Britain**
  https://www.asianrationalist.org.uk/

- **Indian Committee for Scientific Investigation of Claims of the Paranormal**
  http://www.indiansceptic.in/

- **Indian Workers Association (GB)**
  http://iwagb.org/

- **James Randi Educational Foundation**
  https://web.randi.org/

- **Koestler Parapsychology Unit**
  https://koestlerunit.wordpress.com/

- **Ritual Abuse Network Scotland (RANS)**
  https://rans.org.uk/

- **Safe Child Africa**
  https://www.safechildafrica.org/

FURTHER READING

- **Twisted Scriptures: Breaking Free from Churches That Abuse**
  Author: Mary Alice Chrnalogar
  Publisher: Zondervan
  ISBN-13: 9780310234081

- **Ungodly Fear: Fundamentalist Christianity and the Abuse of Power**
  Author: Stephen Parsons
  Publisher: Lion Hudson
  ISBN-13: 9780745942889

- **When Prayer Fails: Faith Healing, Children, and the Law**
  Author: Shawn Francis Peters
  Publisher: Oxford University Press
  ISBN-13: 9780195306354

Printed in Great Britain
by Amazon

30427847R00047